Maxie's Magnificent Adventures

Volume 3

Ed Larson

Authors Note

I write these little stories out of love for Kira, Macy, Evan, and Grayson and yes, for my loyal companion Maxie. You all are wonderful. Each one of you has unique gifts that make you special. It has been and will continue to be a joy for me to watch as these "gifts" reveal themselves as you continue to grow. My hope is that you never stop growing and never stop discovering new "adventures".

Papa Ed

Prologue

It had been nearly three years since Maxie had taken the Grandkids on their first adventure and the memory of those exciting travels had faded in their minds. They had tried many times to convince her to share another fantastic journey with them by grasping her paws and repeating the magic chant "Fumbalar Mondo Tintular Condol". But again and again Maxie did not respond, so that, after a while, they came to believe that those journeys never really happened but were only wonderful dreams they had created and shared in their imaginations. Only Grayson, being the youngest, still held out hope that the adventures were real and that maybe someday they would be able to again travel with Maxie to magical places. He would often lay awake at night and think about his old friend Barney and long for the day that he would see that big black bear and his rabbit pal Roscoe. Little did Grayson know that it would be his unwavering belief in Maxie's power that would bring about a most exciting and dangerous series of adventures for him, his older brother Evan and his two cousins, Kira and Macy.

Every Christmas Eve, Nana and Papa Ed invite the whole family over for dinner and the opening of presents. Nana works the whole week decorating the house for the event and even Papa Ed gets caught up in the spirit of the season and, after his normal grumbling, goes out and finds the tallest tree that will just fit in the house and sets about decorating it, refusing any assistance or taking any advice from Nana. He considers himself a master tree decorator and is resistant to accepting any suggestions. Nana just smiles and goes about her tasks as Papa Ed belts out his own versions of Christmas carols while he dances about decorating with ever increasing intensity. When he's finished, she comes in and steeps heavy praise upon him for another "perfect" tree. Papa Ed is suspicious that she may make minor modifications to his creation in the days leading up to Christmas so he scrupulously conducts a daily inspection and questions any observed changes.

Over the years, a routine has been established for the day with everyone pitching in to make the event special. Drinks and appetizers of all sorts are in abundance and the throng grazes contentedly through the afternoon. The adults stick to the kitchen and living room while the kids all make for the office which also serves as their toy repository. Maxie wanders the premises plying the guests for free hand outs but eventually ends up sharing most of her time with the kids, her favorite companions. Soon it's time for dinner and everyone heaps their plate with goodies from the buffet line and proceeds to stuff themselves. After dinner comes entertainment which consists of the kids singing and Papa Ed's reading of Maxie's annual Christmas Poem. Finally comes the moment the kids have been waiting for. Presents!! And soon the bottom of the tree is vacant and the living room is filled with wrapping paper. While the adults relax in the midst of the mess, the kids head back to the office to check out their newly acquired booty. Of course, Maxie tags along.

As the four grandkids gather in the office to play with their new toys Grayson speaks up and says he wants to try one more time to see if Maxie will take them on another of her adventures. Kira says, "Grayson, I'm too old for those fantasies. Sure, for a while I thought my trip to Catalina riding on top of Dolly the Dolphin was real, but looking back on it now, I'm sure that it was just all in a dream that I had". "I agree with Kira chimed in Macy. Those are good memories of Dolly, Polly, and Captain Bill but we all know that it couldn't really have happened." "Yah" said Evan, "it's time for you to grow up Gray. It was a lot of fun meeting Barney in my dreams but I woke up and realized it was all just my imagination". "Come on guys!" pleaded Grayson, "let's just try one last time and I promise I'll never bother you about it again."

Well, the three felt kind of sorry for Grayson so they said they would give it one last try and all four gathered in a circle with Maxie in the middle, and each took hold of one of her paws. Together, they recited three times the chant that they had almost forgotten. "Fumbalar Mondo Tintular Condol". As they finished, they all looked at Grayson and saw the disappointment on his face because it was clear that nothing strange had happened. "It's OK Gray" said Evan, it's just time to leave those fantasies behind and live in the real world. Look at all these neat presents we've got!" "I guess you're right" said Grayson. "I had just really hoped that it wasn't a dream after all. I don't really feel like playing with this stuff right now. I think I'll just go out to the kitchen and talk to Nana." And he turned to leave the room. It was then that he noticed that the door to the office was closed although he was certain that, before they started the chant, it had been open. Not only that, but the color of the door had changed! It was now a beautiful gold that glistened in the soft light of the office. Emblazoned on the door was the image of a frog in the midst of a giant leap. As he reached for the knob, there came a voice from behind him that loudly exclaimed, "Just exactly where do you think you're going Grayson?

I've got something important that you should all hear. By the way, thanks for believing in me Gray. "The four of them turned and stared in astonishment at Maxie who was standing proudly on the sofa with a huge grin spread across her face and with her tail wagging at warp speed. They slowly knelt down to be at eye level and waited expectantly for Maxie to continue.

"Another Adventure!"

"You will have the opportunity to join with me in a most fantastic journey through time and space, if you think you are up to it.", announced Maxie. "But, before you decide on whether you want to do it, you need to understand some important rules that will govern our travels together. Pay very close attention as your very lives may depend on how well you all can work together within these rules." And so Maxie began.

"There will be four separate adventures along our journey and, for each of these adventures; one of you will be the "Adventure Captain". The Adventure Captain will be granted a magical power that he or she can use within their adventure to help us as we make our way through that adventure and to the next golden door. You will discover what magical power you have been granted only after you pass through the golden door that marks the entrance to each new adventure. There will be a hint of this power engraved on each door. Only the new Adventure Captain can open the golden door that leads from one adventure to the next. Do you all understand so far?" They all nodded that they did so Maxie continued.

"For any one of us to finish the journey safely and capture the magnificent reward that awaits us at the end, we must all finish the journey together. So, as the Three Musketeers used to say "It's all for one and one for all". Except now there is five of us. Now, I need to explain a very important detail. Once an Adventure Captain has opened a golden door leading out of one adventure and into the next, we have only ten seconds to all pass through. After ten seconds the door will slam shut and remain locked forever and, if we all don't pass through, then we will all be trapped forever."

I can't promise that you will survive this fantastic journey but I can promise that you will see wonderful and exciting things beyond your imagination and that, if you work closely as a team, use each Captain's powers wisely, and have some luck, you will complete this journey and capture your reward. So, the time has come for you to decide whether you want to join with me on this quest. Remember, you must all go or none of you can go."

They all looked at one another with questioning eyes, then Kira, being very wise and practical, spoke up. "Excuse me Maxie, but I think we would all like to know a little bit more about what's in store for us in each of these adventures. To be specific, could you please describe what dangers we might encounter and also what this "fantastic reward" is that you alluded to? I for one am not inclined to embark on this journey without knowing this.

Maxie thought this request over for a bit and then cocked her head to the side and explained, "I really don't know what dangers and rewards may await us but that's precisely why this will be a fantastic journey. We will be explorers just like Christopher Columbus and his crew when they sailed off to find the New World. Naturally, they were afraid, but the promise of discovering wonderful places and things helped them overcome their fear and forge ahead. Sometimes we have to take some risk in order to achieve great things. Columbus did and he will forever be remembered throughout history for what he achieved. How about the rest of you? Are you in or out?

Being younger and more adventurous, Macy shouted out "I'm in!! Let's get going." Grayson leapt to his feet, clenched his fist high over his head and yelled "Yah!!" Then they all turned to Evan, who had been pretty quiet. He's a very thoughtful young man and likes to think things through before making decisions, especially big decisions like this one. He slowly stood and addressed the group. "I usually like to do things on my own, but sometimes it's important to be part of a team to get really big things accomplished. This "Journey" sounds like a really big thing and, if we don't take the chance, we may wonder for the rest of our lives about the adventures we missed. I guess what I'm saying is that, I'm in if you are all in."

Apparently, Maxie's "Columbus" analogy had the desired effect as Kira also stood and asked that they all form a circle and hold hands. She then said solemnly, "Let us all join and make a pledge that we will face these adventures together and that we always look out and protect one another as we face the unknown." Maxie looked proudly up at them with a grin on her face as her stubby tail again became a blur. And so their Fantastic Journey began.

Chapter 1

They all turned towards the golden door leading from the office. "What do you think the meaning of that frog is?" asked Kira. "Beats me" said Evan "but I suppose it will become clear when we pass through to the other side." "What are we waiting for?" blurted Macy and rush forward to open the door. She pulled on the knob as hard as she could but it didn't budge. "Wait!" cautioned Kira. "Remember, we all have to be ready to pass through the door within ten seconds so we need to get organized first. Let's line up and then each one of us will try the door. Macy you and Maxie are at the end of the line because we already know you're not the Adventure Captain for this door. I'll try it first, then Evan and finally Grayson. Whoever is successful in opening the door must go through immediately and the rest have to follow right on their tail. Does everyone understand?" The all gave the thumbs up sign and got ready to rush through the door once it opened.

Kira moved forward and gave a firm pull on the knob, but it held fast. Then it was Evan's turn but it resisted his efforts as well. That left only

Grayson. He stepped forward bravely and then turned back to face his companions and said firmly. "Remember, it's all for one and one for all. Now let's do this." He grasped the knob expecting to give it a turn but, as soon as he touched it, the door sprung inward and they were all bathed in a brilliant light. One after the other they stepped through and let out screams as they found themselves falling into a foggy void. They landed with a huge splash in a shallow marsh that was covered with smelly green algae. Luckily, it was shallow enough that they could stand but the bottom was really mucky sort of like it was off the dock at Nana's place in Minnesota.

"This is gross!" yelled Kira. "Yuck" echoed Macy, I got this green stuff all over me." "Let's get out of this swamp" said Evan. "Grayson, you're the Adventure Captain, so how about telling us where to go?" Grayson didn't feel much like a Captain at the moment as he spit out a big mouthful of green slime that he took in when he hit the water. "I feel kind of sick", he moaned and they all thought he looked like he was going to puke. But he didn't.

Meanwhile, Maxie was happily swimming in circles around them. She thought the swamp had a wonderful bouquet of strange new scents to be experienced and was busy cataloging all of them in her mental library. It was only when her concentration was broken by a distant roar from the far side of the swamp that she started making her way towards the nearest dry land. The others were way ahead of her.

"What was that?" whispered Macy. "I don't know" said Evan, "but it sounded really big". "What is this place?" said Kira. "I don't think I want to be here. It's scary." They all looked expectantly at Grayson who looked a little better but was still quite pale. "I don't know where we are any more than you, but the first thing we need to do is get to some higher ground so that we can take a look around. Let's start moving towards that hill over there" and pointed to a small patch of trees atop a small rise about a mile away. It was tough going through the tall grass and at times they lost sight of the trees but they eventually arrived at a small grove of very majestic looking trees like nothing they had seen before.

"Macy, you always like to climb up on things. Why don't you climb up one of these trees and see what you can see?" suggested Kira. "Alright, I'll give it a go" said Macy as she moved to the base of the tallest tree to figure out the best route to the top. There were some sturdy branches to climb but they didn't start until almost 10 feet off the ground so there was no way to get started. Kira made a suggestion. "Why don't we stand on each other's shoulders and then Macy can climb up on all of us to get to the first branch."

Kira formed the base and on her shoulders stood Evan and then Grayson. Slowly, Macy climbed up the backs of the others until finally, standing on Grayson's shoulders, she was able to firmly grasp the lowest branch and pull herself up. She got to her feet and, looking down flashed a smile and gave the team a big thumbs up. Maxie barked excitedly as Macy began scaling the huge tree. She was nearly 100 feet up when she finally paused and looked out over the surrounding landscape. The shock of what she saw nearly caused her to lose her balance and fall.

Dinosaurs!! Hundreds of them spread across a large grassy valley bordered by towering rock cliffs. There were all kinds. A large herd of Brontosaurus was moving slowly in single file in the direction of the swamp. They were lucky that hadn't stumbled into them as they made their way to the trees. They could have been squashed like bugs and not even noticed by those huge beasts. And there were scattered groups of Stegosaurs, with their armored plated body, grazing contentedly in the lush grass. Macy was so stunned that she didn't speak and just stared at the wondrous scene in complete awe.

"Hey, what do you see Macy?" yelled Evan. "Dinosaurs!!" Macy screamed down excitedly. "What did you just say?" questioned Grayson. "I said I see Dinosaurs, and I'm not dreaming!!! I'm going up higher to get a better look". And up she went. As Macy went higher she didn't notice that the branches started to get smaller and some of them were dead. She was just reaching up to grab the next branch when the one she was standing on broke and she found herself hanging 150 feet above the ground with no place to put her feet and lacking the strength to pull herself up. She screamed down, "Help me; I can't hold on much longer, I'm going to fall!"

Kira frantically tried to figure out how they could get up to the first branch so they could climb up and rescue Macy but there was no way. "Hold on Macy!" they all cried out, but they knew she couldn't hold on much longer and they saw no way to stop the tragedy. In his frustration, Grayson started jumping up and down as he screamed, "We've got to save Macy! We've got to save Macy!" They all stared at him in amazement as he jumped higher and higher and suddenly they understood the meaning of the symbol on the golden door. Grayson wasn't thinking about any door. He was just angry that he couldn't do anything to help Macy and the angrier he got, the higher he jumped. It was only when he bumped his head on a branch 50 feet off the ground that he realized his magical power and it brought him a terrific surge of joy and he confidently declared loudly, "I'm coming Macy! I'll save you!"

"To the rescue!"

Grayson quickly studied the maze of branches leading toward the top of the tree and then he saw it, a narrow shaft with no interference from branches that led to the very top. He crouched low and, with a mighty thrust of his legs, launched himself upward. Straining with the last bit of her strength to hold on, Macy looked in astonishment as Grayson flew upward past her and landed gently on a sturdy branch above. Just as her strength gave out, she felt his hands grasp her wrists and pull her up to him. She put her arms around him and gave him a big hug followed by a kiss on the cheek. "You saved my life Gray!" He blushed in embarrassment not having a lot of experience with being kissed by beautiful girls.

Grayson was still trying to compose himself when Macy, undaunted by her brush with death, declared "I'm gonna climb right to the top so I can really get a great look at all those dinosaurs." And up she went. Grayson just rolled his eyes in disbelief. "Don't you ever learn Macy? Please be careful. This is high enough for me." And he turned his eyes out to the magnificent scene in the valley below. Meanwhile, Macy had seated herself on a sturdy branch at the very top and was taking in the view. Below, Evan and Kira were yelling up at the two. "Get down here now before you fall down! We want to hear about what you've seen up there."

With her attention drawn to the many strange and fantastic creatures below, Macy was not aware of the danger that circled high above her. A huge Pterodactyl had spotted her and was gliding silently down to collect a nice little snack for her new born chicks. Her chicks liked to play with their food for a while before devouring it so she had to be careful not to damage this strange little animal. She wanted it to have plenty of spunk when she placed it front of her brood. Before Macy could even grasp what had happened, she felt herself being lifted from her branch and carried off. She looked up in horror into the glaring red eyes of this huge flying beast that was staring down at its freshly caught prey. She could barely manage a scream. "Please save me Grayson!!"

Grayson looked up when he felt the tree shake above him just in time to see his cousin being snatched from her perch. He then heard her screams of terror and watched to see her being carried to what looked like a giant nest high on a rock pinnacle on the far side of the valley. He knew there was no time to waste and jumped down to his companions below. He quickly explained to the others what had happened and told them to head in the direction of the Pterodactyl nest. He then turned and bounded off with leaps that were longer than a football field. In less than a minute he was looking up at the nest and could hear high above the excited chirps of hungry Pterodactyl chicks as well as the terrified screams of Macy who kept shouting. "Please don't eat me!!"

Just then, the mother Pterodactyl left the nest, apparently in search of more food for her ravenous chicks and Grayson knew this was his only chance to attempt a rescue. He leaped straight up the side of the towering pinnacle, over the edge of the large nest, and landed with a thud right next to Macy who was surrounded by four very hungry looking reptilian birds who were delighted to see that and extra course had just been added to their meal. With their beaks snapping menacingly they began closing in on Grayson and Macy who were standing in the midst of a scattered collection of skeletons that was all that remained of previous visitors.

"What do we do now?" Macy pleaded. "Quick, jump on my back!" Grayson commanded and Macy didn't hesitate. In an instant Grayson had vaulted out of the circle of death and landed atop the edge of the nest with Macy gripping him tightly. It wouldn't be long before mama returned so they needed to make their exit quickly. Grayson knew that even with his incredibly strong legs to cushion the impact, there was a good chance they might be badly hurt if he jumped all the way to the ground from such a height. He urgently scanned in all directions and it was then he noticed a small ledge protruding from a sheer rock cliff that was separated from them by a few hundred feet and just slightly below them. And, in the same instant, along the ledge, he saw the entrance to a cave. From the mouth of the cave, came a soft golden glow. Could it be that this cave would lead to a golden door and their escape from this terrifying adventure? With no time to ponder the question, Grayson said, "Hold on tight Macy", as he leapt from the nest and flew across the chasm to land firmly on the rocky ledge. "That's it, I don't want to do this anymore!" cried Macy, as she slid from Grayson's back to stand with wobbly legs on the narrow ledge.

"Hold on!"

Looking down on the plain below, they could see the others making their way through the tall grass in their direction but they also saw something else that alarmed them. Unbeknownst to their companions, they were being followed by a team of Velociraptors who had apparently picked up their scent and were tracking them down. Maxie, who was bringing up the rear, smelled the raptors as well and her warning barks could be heard echoing across the valley floor.

"I'll be back. Stay put" Grayson told Macy and off the ledge he went. In three giant leaps he landed next to the three. "Keep moving to the base of that cliff ahead. There are some nasty critters back here that I need to take care of". He scooped up Maxie and away he bounded in the direction of the raptors. Almost immediately upon landing, he could hear the snarling raptors making their way towards them through the tall grass and slowly begin to encircle them. Maxie was barking wildly as six ferocious looking man sized lizards with huge point teeth emerged from the cover.

"I bet you guys would love to snack on this sweet little dog wouldn't you?" said Grayson as he held out Maxie to the drooling raptors. Maxie stared wide eyed up at Grayson with a look that said, "Have you gone crazy?" The temptation was just too great for the hungry raptors. They all charged at the two with front claws outstretched and teeth gnashing wildly in expectation. Maxie closed her eyes expecting to feel the pain of being torn to shreds and knowing that her "adventure" was about to end. But Grayson was not perturbed and with a slight grin on his face, he catapulted Maxie and himself upward at the last possible moment and took great delight as he looked down to see the raptors drive headlong into one another. He could see a number of large shattered teeth glinting in the sun as they flew through the air from the center of the collision. Leaving the dazed and confused raptors behind, he quickly caught up with others who had just arrived at the base of the cliff. They were shouting up at Macy who was excitedly telling them that she had explored the cave and discovered that indeed, it led to a golden door.

One by one, Grayson took each of them on his back and, with his super powered legs, vaulted to the ledge where Macy was waiting. He brought Maxie up last and she licked his face clean in appreciation of his heroism that saved them all. Then each of the kids in turn went up to Grayson and gave him a big hug and thanked him profusely. Macy then led them to the entrance to the cave and the door which led to the next adventure. Safe at last they thought but were shocked and terrified when they heard the ear splitting screech of a very angry mama Pterodactyl diving to pluck them off the ledge. Without hesitation, they all dove into the narrow opening of the cave. There was just enough room for the Pterodactyl to squeeze through the opening with her wings folded and she slowly advanced on the group with the teeth of her huge beak snapping the air.

Macy was the first to reach the golden door but the others were right on her tail. She tried to open it but it held fast. Then Kira stepped forward and gave it a try but no luck. Just as the giant bird was about to snap up Grayson, Evan touched the knob and the door immediately sprung open and they all scrambled through, leaving behind the frustrated screeching of one very angry Pterodactyl. As they went flying through the door, Kira thought to look at the symbol on the door and was puzzled to see that it looked like the image of a human brain with sparkling lights around it. There was no time to think about what it meant.

Chapter 2

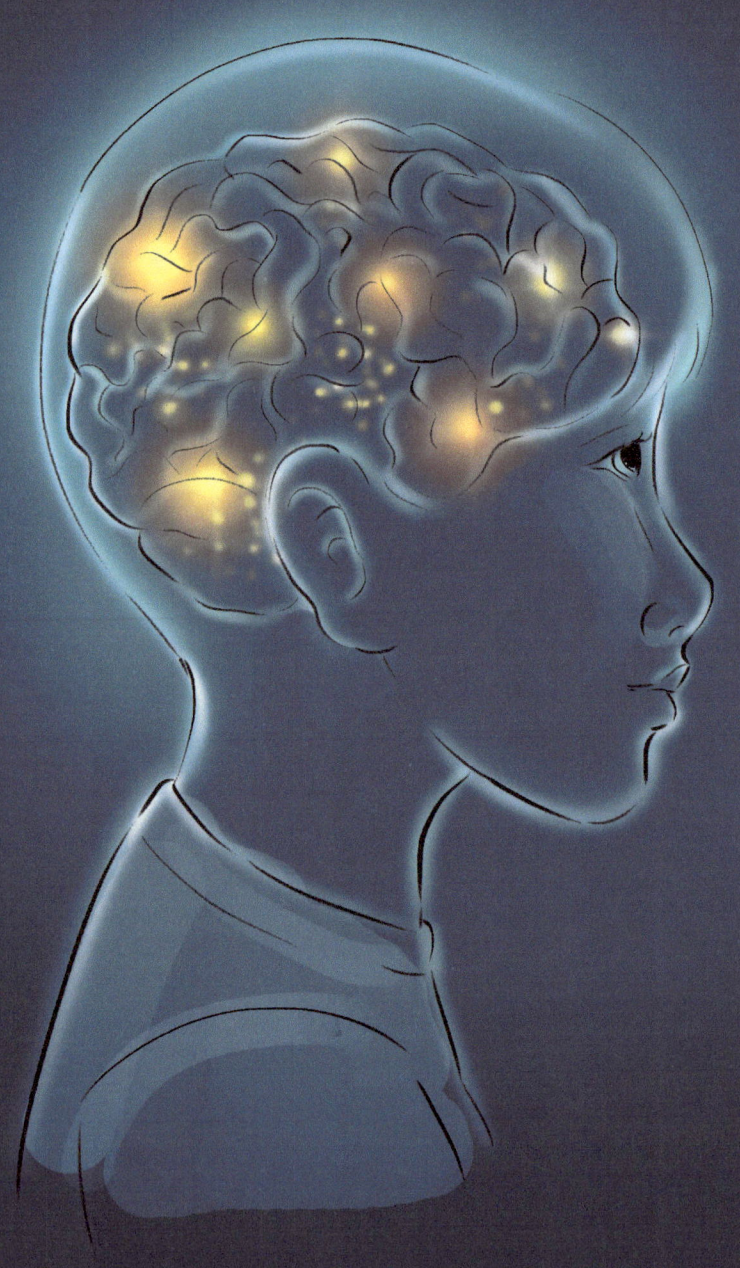

As they plunged through the door, still smelling the hot breath of the Pterodactyl and hearing her beak snapping, they all lost consciousness. When they awoke, they were wedged into a tiny closet like space that felt like it was rolling back and forth and they could hear intermittent loud booms coming from beyond the walls. Macy yelled, "Whoever is laying on me, please get off right now!" Grayson pulled himself upright and was just able to stand without banging his head. "Sorry Macy", he said. Soon they were all standing up, although Kira and Evan had to stoop the clear the low ceiling and Maxie was tangled up at their feet. "Where are we?" asked Kira. Evan calmly pronounced, "Well, judging from the periodic rolling that we feel, I would say that we are on an ocean going vessel of some sort." "Further, given the smell of frying salt pork that I pick up, I would guess that we are very near the galley of a wooden ship." He didn't quite know how he figured all this out so quickly. It just seemed to naturally pop into his head.

"Help! Get us out of here!" shouted Grayson at the top of his lungs. They waited anxiously as they heard someone or something approaching from the other side of one of the walls. Then came the sound of a bolt being slid back and they realized too late that the wall wasn't really a wall but a door. As the door swung open, they all tumbled out onto a hard wooden floor. They looked up to see various dead animals hanging from big iron hooks that came down from the ceiling. There were geese and ducks as well as chickens and rabbits. It was a pretty gruesome sight but not nearly as frightening as the figure that towered over them. He was a huge man with a blood stained apron that had long since forgotten it was supposed to be white. He had a gigantic beard and fierce penetrating eyes. As he brandished a shining meat cleaver over his head he boomed, "Stowaways! I've got stowaways!" In that instant, they all thought they would soon be hanging on the hooks as well. To their relief, this giant, who was apparently the ships cook, lowered his cleaver and then gave them a big grin through a sparse set of brown teeth. "Now just how did you manage to get yourself into my storage locker?" he inquired.

Evan knew there was no way that the truth would work in this situation so he quickly composed a story that they had wandered into the galley when the ship was in port and somehow got stuck in the locker. The cook, whose name was Big John, wasn't buying the story but decided to let it go for now and went about introducing himself to the four stowaways. After the introductions he said, "Well, we need to get you top side and have the Captain get a look at you. I don't think he'll be too happy about having extra mouths to feed. You best be thinking about what work you can do to earn your keep, lest he's liable to toss you overboard." That got their attention and they thought hard as Big John led them to the upper deck.

As they ascended into the bright sunlight they squinted up to see a man on the quarter deck who was obviously the Captain. He was standing ramrod straight with his balance in perfect harmony with the pitching ship. Looking out towards the horizon with his telescope, it was clear from the scowl on his face that he was not a very happy Captain at the moment. Just then there was a big "boom!" as one of the ship's cannons was discharged. Far out on the water floated a bobbing raft with a cloth sheet spread between two vertical poles jutting up from the rafts deck. On the sheet was painted a red bull's eye. Far off to the side of the raft, there erupted a white geyser where the last errant cannon ball struck. "Can't you idiots hit anything? How can we call ourselves a pirate ship with shooting like that? Nobody will fear us. They'll just laugh."

"Captain, may I have a word with you?" asked Big John. "What is it Cookie? Can't you see I'm busy!" he said without even looking down. "We've got a little problem here Captain" said Big John and motioned to the four kids and their dog when the Captain finally looked down at him. "Now just where did you all come from?" he shouted. "As if I don't have enough to worry about, now I've got kids and a dog on my ship. First we can't shoot and now this. If word gets out, we'll be laughed right out of the Caribbean. You four get up here and Cookie, throw that mutt overboard." "Don't you dare hurt our dog!" screamed Macy. "Now a little girl is giving me orders on my ship? The world has gone crazy. OK, just get that little black mutt out of my sight" said the Captain. Big John quickly scooped up Maxie and hustled below decks.

"Now, where were we? Oh yes, you're going to tell me how you came about being on what is supposed to be the most feared pirate ship in the Caribbean." "We will Captain Sir." said Evan respectfully, "But first, would you mind if I gave you some advice on how to improve the accuracy of your cannon fire?" "What?" he bellowed. "First I have this little thing, what's your name?" "I'm Macy" she responded. He continued. "I have Macy here giving me orders on my own ship and how I have, and what's your name?" "Evan" he replied. "I have Evan ready to teach my crew how to fire our cannon! What's next? Are you going to tell me how to trim my sails?" "Well, said Evan, I actually do have an idea on how you might be able to add a few more knots to your top speed with a modification to your sail setup, but let's first address your crews poor shooting skill." "Well by all means Mr. Evan, please go about explaining what we must do in order to at least get close to that target out there" said the Captain sarcastically. "By the way, my name is Captain Bill and I was once the most feared pirate in these parts but my reputation has slipped a bit lately and who might these two be?" Kira and Grayson stepped forward and introduced themselves. Captain Bill reached out and gave each of them a firm handshake. "OK Evan, it's time for you to give us a gunnery lesson." he chuckled.

As Evan stood in front of the gun crews he felt a flood of knowledge enter his mind. At his command were all the complex ballistics equations developed by the most brilliant mathematicians who ever lived. He was able to instantly compute drag coefficients, propellant thrust values, gravitational impact, wind effects, and launch angles; and precisely determine cannon ball trajectories. He even calculated the effects of the ship's and target raft's roll characteristics as well as the impact of the earth's rotation on the trajectory, known as the Coriolis Effect. This mathematics was far too complex to be understood by the sailors so he took the results of the calculations he performed within his computer like brain and reduced it to relatively simple instructions as to elevation and azimuth angles and powder charge. He then stood behind one of the gun crews and supervised the setup of their cannon. At the precise moment his calculations predicted the highest probability of hit, he shouted "Fire" and the crew touched off the cannon. To everyone's astonishment, except Evan's, the ball flew squarely through the center of the target. The entire crew erupted in an ear splitting cheer.

"Hip Hip Hooray! Hip Hip Hooray! Hip Hip Hooray!" Captain Bill was dumbstruck with astonishment. He quickly gained his composure and, smiling down at Evan, pronounced "Looks like we're going to regain some respect around these parts. You need to explain how exactly you pulled off this magic. I would be honored if you and your companions joined me for dinner in my cabin, and yes, you can bring that little mutt along."

As they walked down to the quarters the Captain had instructed be prepared for them, Kira turned to Evan and asked, "How did you do that up there? It was unbelievable!" Evan said, "It seemed to come so naturally. I just was able to figure it all out." Then Kira remembered the symbol on the golden door and understood what it meant and described to Evan what she had seen. "I guess you have a super brain Evan. It must contain all the knowledge that has been learned by the all smartest people who ever lived. That's really impressive. I don't think you'll be having much trouble in school". They all laughed at that.

That evening they enjoyed a wonderful dinner that Big John prepared especially for them. The main course was one of the chickens they had seen hanging in the galley. Big John had cooked it in a big iron pot and seasoned it with his secret recipe of onions, herbs, spices and seaweed. There was also fresh grilled seafood which they all gobbled hungrily except Macy, who unfortunately has a seafood allergy. She had two helpings of chicken instead. Fresh vegetables were especially rare on the old sailing ships but Big John pulled out all the stops for the kids. Evan was pleasantly surprised to see fresh steamed broccoli on the table, and, although it wasn't prepared in the special way that his Nana did it, it was delicious. He felt a bit guilty about eating so much of the rare treat, but Big John and Captain Bill urged him on. The kids had burned up a lot of energy dodging dinosaurs and they were famished. Now they were pleasantly stuffed.

Captain Bill offered them all a mug of grog after the meal but they told him they were still too young to drink alcohol. He laughed at that, as it was quite normal for young cabin boys to share libations with the older crew members. But he accepted their decision and had Big John bring out a couple coconuts that they had collected at a small island on their route. He took a curved blade from a scabbard on his waist and used it to carve a small hole in each of the coconuts and poured the sweet coconut juice out into four small cups. He then raised his grog in a toast to the four adventurers. "To my new young friends and of course to their pal Maxie". They all clinked glasses and enjoyed their liquid dessert.

Captain Bill then turned to Evan and asked: "Do you think you could write down an explanation of what you did that caused that cannon ball to hit dead center?" "No problem", said Evan. "Just bring me paper and pen and I'll do it right now." Captain Bill retreated quickly and was back immediately with sheets of parchment, a feathered pen, and a small bottle of ink. Evan went to work while the others at the table watched intently, none understanding in the least the complex equations and procedures he was writing. In less than fifteen minutes Evan passed two filled sheets of parchment to Captain Bill and proclaimed: "That should do it. I've simplified it a bit but, if your gun crews follow these instructions and use these equations, they'll be the best shots on the high seas by far." Captain Bill was so overcome with the realization that his ship would again achieve the respect he sought that he leapt to his feet and gave Evan a big hug followed by a hearty slap on the back. "Thank you Evan my boy! You'll never know how much this means to me. Please tell me if there is anything that I can do for you and your friends in return for this marvelous gift.

Evan became thoughtful for a moment and then spoke. "Your hospitality has been wonderful Captain Bill and we would love to stay on with you as you once again become the most feared pirate in the Caribbean. But we must get back to our home and, to do that, we must find a golden door that leads from this adventure into the next. Have you heard about or seen any such thing in your travels?" At this, Captain Bill's eyes widened in excitement and he bolted from the room. Upon his return, he ordered the table be cleared and he spread out a large map. "A beggar on the streets in Port Elizabeth sold this to me for one doubloon. I was sure it wasn't worth anything but I felt sorry for the old man. I couldn't figure out how to read the map so I just tossed in aside, but when you said "golden door", it jogged my memory and look here." He pointed to a mountainous island in a chain of islands and there at the top of the highest peak was the symbol of a crude door that had been painted gold. "The problem is, I can't tell from this map where this island is. Nothing looks familiar to me but, if you think this might help you find your way home, you are welcome to have it." With that, he rolled the map up and handed it to Evan who received it graciously and tucked it inside his waistband. "Thanks Captain Bill, I'll study this more closely later and maybe I can figure it out. Right now I think I would like to take a stroll up on the deck. That was a great meal you had prepared for us. Our thanks to you and Big John. You guys want to join me?" The other three nodded in agreement and, with a few groans, were able to raise themselves and their full bellies from the table.

It was pleasant topside. The sun was setting in the West creating a golden glow across the water and a freshening breeze caressed their faces. As they circled the vessel, Maxie just had to show off as she pranced along the top of the railing just like she always did on Papa Ed's fishing boat back in Minnesota. Not to be outdone, Grayson felt like it was time to once again demonstrate his amazing leaping ability. He stood on the railing and prepared to launch himself up to one of the yardarms high above the deck confident that he could easily vault the thirty feet to his landing spot. "Hey watch this everybody!" and they all turned to see him crouch deeply and catapult himself upward. With shocked horror they saw that Grayson only rose far enough in the air to clear the railing and then, with a frantic scream, he fell to waves below.

There was no hesitation by Maxie as she leaped from the railing to rescue her friend. In short order she was followed by the other three. They swam in widening circles in search of Grayson but the swells made it difficult to see any distance and their shouts were not being answered. At last, Evan crested a wave and saw his brother struggling to stay afloat in the ever roughening water. He arrived at his side just in time to grasp Grayson's arm as he slipped under. "I've got you Gray!" he said and then yelled for the others. Soon, the four were clustered in a small circle treading water while Maxie swam protectively around them. They looked in dismay as the ship sailed off, their shouts for help unheard in the sharpening wind. "Now what do we do?" pleaded Macy. "I can't keep this up much longer."

It was then that Kira noticed the raft that the pirates had been using to carry their gunnery targets. It was attached to the ship by a long rope. In all the excitement of their arrival, the crew had apparently forgotten to bring the raft back onboard. That oversight gave them hope, but it wouldn't be long until the raft would leave them behind just as the ship had. They had to start swimming fast! Being the strongest swimmer, Maxie reached the raft first and climbed aboard and, after a quick shake, turned to see how the others were progressing. It was going to be close but it looked like they would all make it before the raft passed them.

Then she saw it! Coming up behind the four was the black silhouette of a large dorsal fin breaking the surface and trailing a white foam streak as it closed on its prey. Maxie began barking a loud warning to the others which caused Macy, who was at the end of the pack, to quickly turn. Her eyes widened in fright as she saw what was approaching. "Shark!!" she screamed and with a burst of energy was immediately leaving the others behind. Maxie could see they wouldn't be able to reach the raft before one or more of them were taken by the killer fish. Demonstrating the loyalty and bravery that would make any dog envious, Maxie sprang from the raft and paddled into the face of danger. She met the kids and they were amazed to see her keep right on going without hesitation. Her job was to protect her friends no matter what.

The Great White sensed and then saw the little black dog coming its way and was confused. It was used to its prey trying to escape or at least being paralyzed with fear but this little creature was doing neither. The shark slowed and began circling Maxie trying to figure out this mystery. Soon it became convinced there was nothing to fear and made its charge. Meanwhile, the kids had made it to the raft and had all turned to see what they feared would be the end for Maxie. They screamed, "Look out Maxie" just as the huge fish launched itself at the struggling black dog. Miraculously, the shark missed, passing just underneath Maxie who slid down the back of the shiny beast and managed to grab a big mouthful of dorsal fin as she did. The shark dove under with Maxie still holding on tight. A minute later the shark surfaced near the raft with a mighty leap in an effort to rid itself of its unwanted passenger. It worked. When the shark crashed to the surface, Maxie was knocked loose and floated to the surface dazed and disoriented. "Swim Maxie!!" they all cried as they saw the dorsal fin, now with a big piece missing, closing on their friend. With the last of her strength, Maxie struggled mightily to cover the few feet to the raft. Kira reached down and plucked her up just as the Great White surfaced with its jaws of death sprung wide open. The razor sharp teeth snapped shut just missing its prey but closing on the rope that that led to the ship, neatly severing it. The all stared in dismay as the ship's sails began to fade into the dusk.

As darkness came, they all huddled closely at the center of the raft. Kira had taken down the big canvas that had served as a target and, except for the hole in the middle where Evan's cannon shot had passed; it was in perfect condition and served as both a tent and blanket for the group. "We need to get some rest and tomorrow we need to figure out how we are going to get out of this mess", advised Evan. They all murmured their agreement. Too tired to contemplate the dangers they had overcome and the challenges yet ahead, they were soon fast asleep with Maxie curled in their midst.

It was mid morning when they awoke to a cacophony of squawking shore birds that circled inquisitively overhead. Evan knew immediately this was a positive sign and instructed everyone to scan the horizon for land and after a few seconds it was Macy who spotted the tiny outline of a distant island. "I see land!" she screeched and the others quickly turned their heads to see where she was pointing and, sure enough, they could all see it too. Evan made a rapid assessment of the wind direction and the prevailing current and, with their makeshift sail in place and some hand paddling by the entire crew, they made steady progress towards the island and what they hoped was safety.

As the island gradually came into view, Evan suspected this might be the same island that had appeared on the map given to him by the Captain. He pulled the map from his waistband and after comparing the topography of the island and the surrounding smaller islands with the depictions on the map, his suspicion was confirmed. They were coming to the island that he believed held the next golden door! He excitedly shared his conclusions with the others and was rewarded with thankful smiles all around. Maxie just wagged her appreciation.

With a favorable breeze and some excited paddling, in a few hours they had arrived at a gently sloping beach on the east side of the island. Evan quickly confirmed that the mountain top they were looking for was on the west side, so they were faced with a decision. Either they could stick to the beach and walk around the island or they could head cross country through the thick foreboding jungle that lay in front of them. With some quick calculations he figured it was about 2 miles going the direct route compared with 4 or 5 miles traveling on the beach around the north end of the island. The beach looked like easy walking and they all remembered their time in the jungle dodging dinosaurs, so the vote for the beach route was unanimous. They would soon come to regret that decision.

They hadn't traveled more than a half a mile along the beach when they started having a strange feeling that they were being watched.

Even Maxie was noticeably on edge. Surprisingly, the feeling was emanating from the ocean and not the jungle. They all strained to see the danger their instincts knew was lurking, but there was nothing to be seen but a gentle shore break. And then Grayson saw them!

Pairs of thin periscopes dotted the surface not more than fifty feet from the shore. There were dozens of them and each shaft was topped by a small gray eye that seemed to be focused on their every move. Grayson just had time to sound the alarm when, out of the waves came a huge and ugly, crab like thing. It was right out of a horror movie. Others followed. Each was at least six feet wide with two large pincers and a gaping mouth that looked like it could easily swallow Maxie whole. Along with their periscope eyes, which sat well above their armored body, there were six more eyes arranged across their squatty torso. As they moved towards the terrified group, the "shick, shick, shick" of their pincers grew louder and louder with their anticipation of a hearty meal.

As one, the group turned to make their escape into the jungle but it was then they realized why the crab creatures had chosen this spot to make their attack. Their way was blocked by vertical wall of stone that was at least one hundred feet high. They instinctively looked up and down the beach for an escape only to see, to their dismay, scores of the monsters coming ashore and joining with their brethren to form an ever shrinking semi circle around the panicking band. "Snick, snick, snick" as the circle tightened. Maxie stood in front of the trembling foursome barking and growling, but the advancing horde paid her little heed. As they backed up steadily, Grayson stumbled and looked down to see that he had tripped on a human skull that was half buried in the sand. In fact the base of the cliff was littered with the bleached bones of others who had been caught in the creatures' trap.

Evan quickly assessed their predicament and realized they had only one chance to survive and they would have to move quickly. The creatures had concentrated on their flanks to prevent an escape on the beach but in so doing had thinned their ranks between their victims and the ocean but those gaps were gradually being closed. Once closed, there would be no chance for escape.

Evan shouted "Follow me and I mean now!" and he ran full speed towards the widest gap. The others followed instinctively except for Maxie who didn't think it made much sense running in the direction of those ugly critters. The approaching crabs were momentarily confused by the sight of their victims rushing headlong towards them and hesitated just long enough for the troupe to skirt their way through the gap just barely out of reach of the deadly pincers. Now on the outside of the circle with their backs to the sea, Macy asked "Now what!?" as they watch the lumbering giants turn back towards them and advance steadily. "Now we swim!" exclaimed Evan. He knew crustaceans couldn't swim so they only needed to make it to deeper water in order to be safe, at least temporarily. Fortunately, they were all strong swimmers so, very quickly, they were far enough out to be safe. Once again, Maxie knew what she had to do. The kids needed a diversion in order to make their escape.

All the giant crabs had turned to look out towards their escaping meal. Maxie took this opportunity to make her escape and ran right up over the top of the nearest creature, barely avoiding its outstretched claws as she tumbled to the sand on the outside of the circle. She quickly recovered and faced the monsters who were eying her hungrily. They were slow and she was fast so Maxie thought this would be a good time to have a little fun with these creatures that, for the moment, had lost interest in the swimmers.

Maxie quickly darted back and forth in front of the advancing crab creatures, taunting them with her barks and occasional summersault. With her back turned, she pretended not to see as one lumbered within pincer reach, and then, at the last moment, she jumped to the side as the pincers closed on thin air with a loud "snick". The kids watched intently as they treaded water and soon it became apparent what Maxie was up to.

She was gradually luring the herd back south along the beach so that the adventurers could get back to shore and escape to the north, in the direction of the mountain they sought. Once they made it to shore and had the creatures behind them, they could easily outrun the creatures on the beach. Maxie continued her diversion and it wasn't long before the last crab had moved clear of their path as it brought up the rear of the herd of crab creatures in their relentless pursuit of the little black dog. They quickly made it ashore and began running northward along the beach, no longer noticed by the clawed monsters. They were all worried about what would happen to Maxie but there was little they could do for her at the moment.

In less than an hour, they had made their way to the West side of the island where they stood at the base of a towering peak that seemed to rise up from the beach. At first, there was no apparent route leading up but upon closer inspection it was Macy who noticed a narrow ledge that appeared to zigzag across the sheer rock face. It looked to be no more than a foot wide and even narrower in places. The thought of making their way upward to the dizzying heights along that path made them all turn pale but they knew they had little choice if they were to reach the golden door the map promised. They all faced one another for a brief moment, nodded in unison with grim smiles and turned to begin the climb with Macy leading the way.

The going was tough and hot without a few near falls to the beach far below, but eventually they came to the mouth of a cave. The cave did not appear to be very deep and, as they peered into the dim light of the passageway, they could just make out the silhouette of what looked like a door but, to their dismay, it was obvious that this was not a golden door. They slowly moved forward, and upon closer examination, discovered the door was just a plain old wooden door that appeared to be on the verge of rotting off its hinges. They turned and looked expectantly at Evan who began trying to figure out what this meant.

Evan moved back to the light at the cave entrance where he took out the map and searched it thoroughly for clues. It was then that he noticed something that had escaped his attention earlier. He abruptly slapped his forehead, startling the others. "Of course, it's so obvious! How could I have missed this?" He excitedly invited them gather around him as he placed the map on the ground and began his explanation.

"First let me orient this map properly for you. We are right here." He said as he indicated a spot on the west side of the peak they had just climbed. "As you look out to the sea, that is west and as you look to your right up the beach. That's north, the way we came. Now, do you see on the map this faint golden line that is coming from the west right to this spot where the golden door is shown? I'm pretty sure that is supposed to be a ray of sunlight. So, my guess is, when the sun gets to just the right place in the western sky, it will illuminate the inside of the cave and that old wooden door. What happens then is anybody's guess. Now I need to do some quick calculations." With that, he turned from the group and began staring blankly out to sea while performing some very advanced mathematics in his head.

Evan turned back to the others and said, "I think I've figured it out. When we were on the deck of the pirate ship, I asked the ship's navigator if

I could use his sextant, and I took some quick readings on the stars. Fortunately, it was a nice clear night so I had all the stars I needed for my calculation of the ships latitude and longitude. Of course, when we went overboard, things got a little more complicated. I estimated our direction and distance from the ships last location to this island taking into account wind direction, the ocean currents and a rough estimate of our speed over the water. Anyway, I've got a pretty good idea of our present longitude and latitude here and, knowing the day of the year, I can easily figure out the sun angle relative to the horizon for any time of the day. So, with that, I can figure the exact time that the sun will be located in the sky where it will shine right down the mouth of this cave and onto that old wooden door. By my calculations, that will be exactly 4:30pm which is only about thirty minutes from now. Knowing the rotation speed of the earth and the width and depth of the cave which I've estimated to be 8 feet and 30 feet respectively, I figure the door will be fully illuminated for only about 2 minutes. " As Evan looked at his companions, he could see they were all astounded with his ability to figure this all out. He just murmured sheepishly, "I don't know how I did it. Like I said, all this stuff just seemed to come to me naturally". They were all very glad that it did.

At this moment, it was Grayson who spoke that, which was on all their minds. "We can't leave without Maxie!" With that, they all looked down at the beach from the mouth of the high cave and what they saw made a tremor of worry pass among them. The water, which had been at least 100 feet from the base of the rock cliff, was now within just a few feet. The tide was rising! They knew Maxie would rely on her keen sense of smell to find them, but even Maxie couldn't follow their trail through water. They turned back again to Evan to seek his advice, except for Grayson, who had quickly assessed the situation and decided what he needed to do. Before the others realized he was gone, Grayson had climbed halfway down the rock face and a few minutes later was on the beach and running back in the direction they had come as fast as he could. All the others could do was watch as Grayson disappeared around a bend in the shoreline still running at top speed. Kira shouted after him. "Hurry Grayson, we have less than thirty minutes to escape."

Grayson rounded the north end of the island where he was disheartened to discover that the rising tide had completely covered the tracks they had made on the sandy beach on their escape from the crab creatures. Without tracks to follow, Maxie would never be able to find them in time. Grayson kept running desperately along the route they had passed until he reached a point where the water covered the entire beach. Completely exhausted, he stopped and looked helplessly at the obstacle before him as he tried to catch his breath. He felt the tears come to his eyes with the realization that he may never see his little friend again. It was at this instant that he heard a familiar but distant bark that had to be Maxie's. Sure enough, as he strained to find the source of the bark, he saw Maxie on the far side of the water obstacle. She had her back to Grayson and was barking wildly at the slowly but steadily advancing pack of crab monsters.

Grayson shouted at the top of his lungs. "Maxie, Maxie, Maxie, come on girl! This way!" Maxie momentarily stopped her barking and cocked her head to the side in an attempt to better hear what she had hoped she heard and, when Grayson repeated his call, her hope was realized. She whirled around in the direction of the shouts and could just make out Grayson. He was continuing to shout encouragement while he jumped up and down waving his arms wildly over his head. Maxie was so happy to see her friend that she momentarily forgot about the danger advancing towards her. The loud "snick, snick, snick" behind her quickly brought her back to reality. Those threats and the joy of seeing Grayson provided ample motivation for Maxie to swim as fast as she had ever swum. She launched herself in the direction of her friend.

As Maxie approached, Grayson could hardly contain his happiness at the prospect of having his little pal back at his side. Unfortunately, his spirits were soon dampened. Undaunted by the relatively shallow water obstacle, the crabs continued their relentless pursuit of a meal. Their enthusiasm heightened by the prospect of having this little boy added to the menu. With just the tops of their backs visible in the rising water, they were able to scuttle along the bottom at a speed fast enough to close the gap between themselves and the swimming dog. In fact, the lead crab was nearly within a claws reach of Maxie as she emerged from the water. There was no time for a reunion. Grayson shouted, "Let's go Maxie", and together they began running back along the beach as fast as Grayson's weary legs could move. On the beach, it was easy to outpace the crabs so pretty soon there was a relatively comfortable distance between the pair and their pursuers. They would need every inch of it.

Rounding the last turn on the beach, Grayson was overjoyed to see the familiar peak rising just up ahead. But was shocked to see the water had continued to rise and now covered the entire beach right up to the base of the cliff that led up to the cave. Fortunately, it was at this moment he heard the shouts of encouragement coming down to him from the mouth of the cave. "Come on Grayson! Come on Maxie! Hurry, we've only got five minutes!" Into the water they went with the lead crab monster not more than 100 feet behind them. They only had about the length of a football field to reach the path leading upward to safety but it was tough walking for Grayson in the waist deep water. Fortunately, Maxie was able to easily keep up, swimming alongside him. It seemed like forever, but soon they were at the spot where the path upward began. Grayson lifted Maxie up and placed her on the rock ledge and then began pulling himself up and out of the surf. He was nearly up when suddenly he felt his right foot catching on something.

Grayson looked back over his shoulder and saw in horror that his boot was clamped securely in the outstretched pincer of the ravenous crab. Grayson struggled to hold on the ledge but could feel his strength waning as the creature tried to pull him towards his cavernous mouth, which now appeared to turn up in a malevolent smile as rivulets of drool ran from its corners. Maxie barked in frustration with her inability to free Grayson. Grayson looked up at Maxie with total fear and pleading in his eyes and in that instant Maxie realized what she must do. Her hope was, by jumping into the mouth of the monster, it would loosen its grip on Grayson. Her sacrifice might save her friend. She crouched to make the final leap of her life when she heard it.

From high above came a shout from Evan. "Look out below!" About the time the shout arrived, so did a basketball sized boulder that crashed squarely into the center of the crabs broad back. The brittle shell shattered and huge globs of reddish brown insides came spewing out of the cracks. It smelled awful! As one, all the crab's eyes rolled back in their sockets and its grip on Grayson's boot loosened. By this time, the other crabs had reached them but were temporarily distracted as they devoured their fallen comrade. Maxie and Grayson began scrambling up to the others.

The sun had reached the point that Evan had predicted and the inside of the cave was being bathed in increasing light as the sun sank into the western sky. It was Macy who first noticed when the light reached the bottom of the old wooden door and began transforming it. Where the sun struck the door it appeared the door turned into gold, but on closer examination Macy discovered that it was the same wooden door. Somehow the light made it appear as if it were golden. As the light slowly moved up the door, it revealed lettering that had not previously been visible. The inscription read:

This Door it will open

And allow you to pass

If there's one amongst you

With a Shadow to cast

By this time, Maxie and Grayson had reached the entrance to the cave and, although gasping, Grayson still managed to blurt out, "Evan, you could have killed us with that rock!" Evan replied, "Not a chance, I figured out the precise trajectory so you were in no danger. Besides, you were about to be lunch for that crab in case you've forgotten." "OK, you're right and thanks Bro." He went to his brother to give him a hug but Evan said, "No time. The sun will only illuminate the door for a very short time so we've got to move." They took one last glance down and saw the crabs assembled in a tight semi circle around the base of the path. It was now high tide but they were still visible, and the kids all knew there would be no escaping in that direction.

As they all approached the door, they were amazed to see how bright the inside of the cave had become. The door was absolutely shimmering in gold and the message Macy had discovered stood out clearly. Evan stood in front of the door and inspected it closely. There was no apparent knob or handle. He knew they now had less than two minutes to figure this out and unless, they could pass through this door now, they were doomed. What he hadn't told the others was, based upon his calculations; there was only this one day in year that the sun angle was perfectly aligned with the cave such that the door would be fully illuminated. With their only escape blocked by the monsters below, they were out of options. The seconds seemed to fly by as they all waited for Evan to save them but he wasn't making any progress. Suddenly, he looked at the door and shouted and waved his arms in frustration, "I can't figure this out!" It was then he saw it, or more accurately, he didn't see it. He had waved his arms about but there was no shadow cast on the door. In fact, with Maxie and all the others huddled around him anxiously, there should have been a lot of shadows on that door but there were none.

Without time to explain as the sun continued to set, he told everyone to quickly line up at the door except for Kira and Macy. They did so and, sure enough, the sun seemed to pass through all of them as there were no shadows on the door. He knew the next Adventure Captain had to be Kira or Macy so he motioned Kira to step in front of the door and, when she did, no shadow was cast. That decided it. "Get ready everyone! We've only got 10 seconds to all get through once the door opens so join hands and Grayson, grab hold of Maxie. OK Macy, you're the one. Step in front of the door."

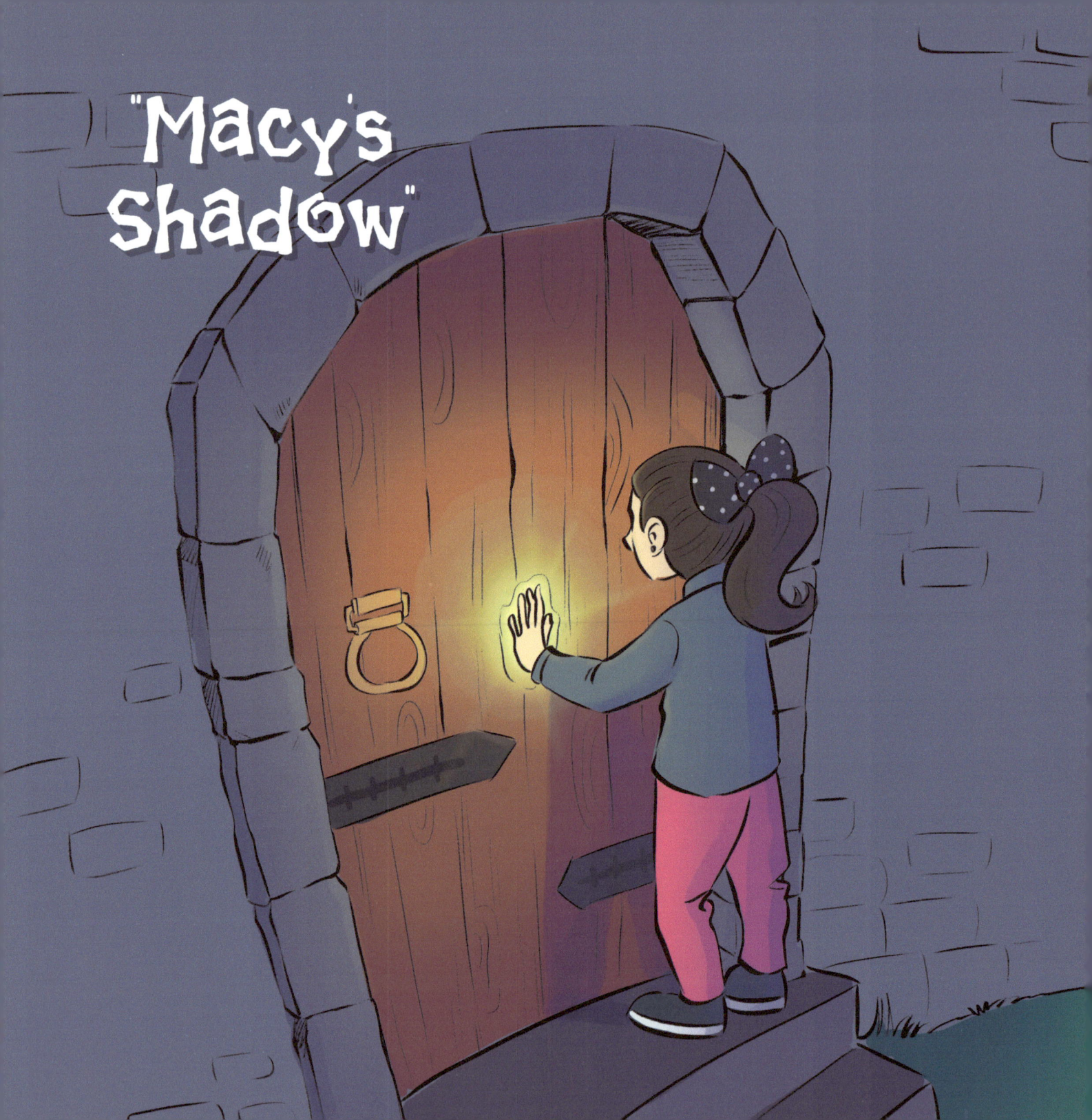

As Macy moved in front of the door, her shadow was cast on its surface and, in that shadow there appeared the imprint of a human hand. As if she knew exactly what this meant, Macy instinctively reached out and firmly pressed her left hand into the imprint. With that, there came a loud creaking as the door slowly moved inward. There could be no hesitation! As soon as the opening was wide enough Macy slipped through, followed by Grayson and Maxie and then Kira. Finally, Evan passed through just as the door began closing. He turned briefly to examine the back of the door and saw what appeared to be a big cat running at top speed. He had just enough time to think "cheetah" and then he was falling into the darkness.

CPSIA information can be obtained
at www.ICGtesting.com
Printed in the USA
BVHW020956010819
554876BV00002B/17/P